MSU
For All Seasons

MICHIGAN STATE UNIVERSITY ALUMNI ASSOCIATION

Eighteen men assembled in East Lansing on November 11, 1868 and held the preliminary meeting of the Michigan Agricultural College Alumni Association. A.J. Cook was elected chairman, and officers and a constitutional committee were selected. One year later, the Alumni Association adopted its first constitution citing its purpose to "strengthen the mutual friendship of the Alumni" and "promote the usefulness of our Alma Mater."

From this meager start, the Michigan State University Alumni Association (MSUAA) has engaged alumni for 140 years, striving to strengthen the life-long connection between alumni and their alma mater. The MSUAA enriches the lives of thousands of alumni, friends, students, and community members through diverse programs, special events, effective communication and networking opportunities.

Over the decades, Michigan State University has been transformed into a premier land-grant institution and one of the top 100 global universities in the world. The current student body totals more than 46,000, with students from all 50 states and 130 other countries. There are more than 470,000 living alumni worldwide. The global Spartan network is vast and the Alumni Association helps connect Spartans around the world.

The motto of the Alumni Association is "Stay Connected," encouraging all alumni to remain engaged with the university throughout their lifetime. *MSU For All Seasons* was created to enhance this mission. These images encompass the spirit of every Spartan. Memories of Michigan State University begin with the magnificent beauty of the campus. All who attend appreciate the people, the events, and the academic experiences that uniquely transform their lives. The fabric of Spartan life is colorful, illuminating, and diverse.

Once you experience the beautiful imagery on these pages, you will want to recapture your personal MSU memories. The Alumni Association invites all alumni and friends to engage and strengthen your Spartan connection at www.msualum.com.

MSU ALUMNI ASSOCIATION
242 Spartan Way
East Lansing, Michigan 48824

(877) MSU-ALUM   (517) 355-8314   www.msualum.com

MSU
For All Seasons

G. L. Kohuth

MICHIGAN STATE UNIVERSITY
ALUMNI ASSOCIATION

We wish to thank the following photographers:

Cammie Cantrell   Brian McNea
Bruce Fox   Tim Potter
Erin Doyle Groom   Harley Seeley
G.L. Kohuth   Kurt Stepnitz
Amanda Ross   Derrick L. Turner
Bruce VandenBerg

Cover photo: Bruce Fox

For additional information about photographs:

*   Michigan State University Alumni Association
    242 Spartan Way, East Lansing, Michigan 48824
    (877) MSU-ALUM (517) 355-8314 www.msualum.com

*   University Relations
    Marketing and Creative Services
    302 Olds Hall, East Lansing, Michigan 48824
    (517) 355-7505 www.ur.msu.edu

Published by

dsa
Publishing & Design Inc.

203 W. Belmont Drive
Allen, Texas 75013
972-747-7866
FAX 972-747-0226
www.dsapubs.com

Publisher: Duff Tussing

Associate Publisher: Steve Boston

Design: Donnie Jones, The Press Group

All images in this book have been reproduced with the knowledge and prior
consent of the photographer and no responsibility is accepted by the producer,
publisher, or printer for any infringement of copyright or otherwise arising from
the contents of this publication. Every effort has been made to ensure that
credits accurately comply with the information supplied.

Printed in the United States

PUBLISHER'S DATA

MSU For All Seasons

Library of Congress Control Number: 2008905561

ISBN Number: 978-0-9818229-1-4

First Printing 2008

10 9 8 7 6 5 4 3 2 1

Kurt Stepnitz

CONTENTS

Derrick L. Turner

Harley Seeley

G. L. Kohuth

Kurt Stepnitz

MICHIGAN STATE
UNIVERSITY

fall

Tim Potter

Derrick L. Turner

Kurt Stepnitz

Harley Seeley

MSUAA Photo

Kurt Stepnitz

Brook Lodge Hotel and Conference Resort
G. L. Kohuth

Kathleen and Milton Muelder Japanese Garden
Harley Seeley

MSU, *we love thy shadows ...*

Tim Potter

Linton Hall
Harley Seeley

G. L. Kohuth

Derrick L. Turner

Wharton Center for Performing Arts
Kurt Stepnitz

Harley Seeley

Harley Seeley

Cyclotron Labaratory
G. L. Kohuth

Opposite Page *Alumni Memorial Chapel*
Erin Doyle Groom

Biomedical and Physical Sciences
Harley Seeley

Linton Hall
Tim Potter

Kurt Stepnitz

Harley Seeley

Spartan Stadium
Harley Seeley

G. L. Kohuth

Auditorium
Tim Potter

Yakeley and Gilchrist Halls
G. L. Kohuth

John A. Hannah
Administration Building
Derrick L. Turner

The Henry Center for
Executive Development
Harley Seeley

Tim Potter

MSU Union
Tim Potter

Harley Seeley

Jenison Fieldhouse

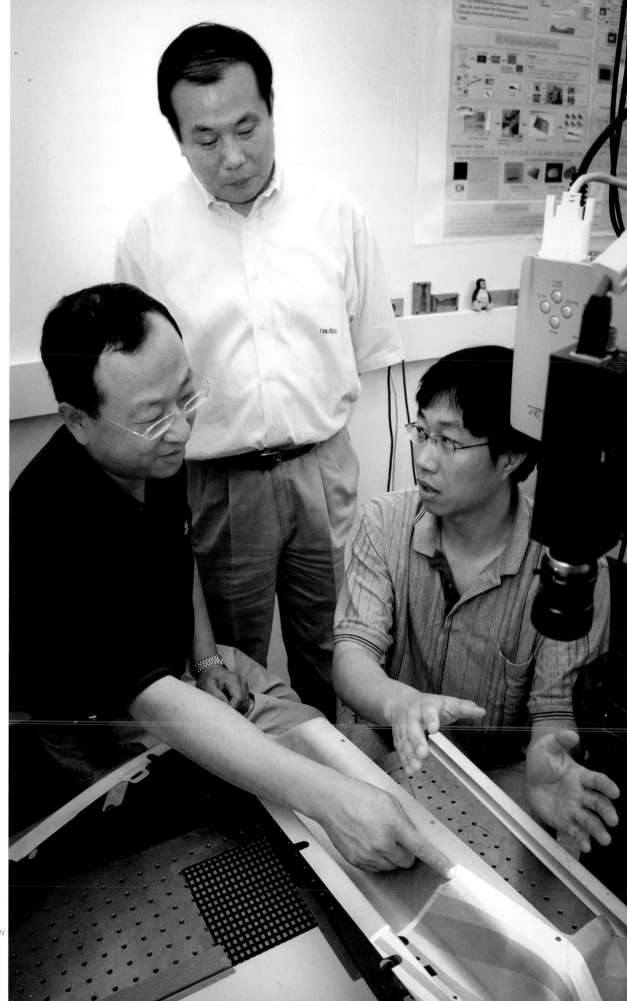

Harley Seeley

MSUAA Photo

O'er ivy covered halls; ...

ain Library
rley Seeley

Williams Hall

Kellogg Hotel and Conference Center
Kurt Stepnitz

Derrick L. Turner

Williams Hall
Tim Potter

Harley Seeley

Kurt Stepnitz

Kurt Stepnitz

Harley Seeley

To give our faith so true, ...

Kurt Stepnitz

Derrick L. Turner

MSU Union
Kurt Stepnitz

MSUAA Photo

Harley Seeley

"Cold War"
October 6, 2001
MSU v. U of M
World Record Attendance 74,554
Erin Doyle Groom

MICHIGAN STATE UNIVERSITY
winter

G. L. Kohuth

Harley Seeley

Sing our love for Alma Mater ...

Red Cedar River
Harley Seeley

MSUAA Photo

Williams Hall
Derrick L. Turner

Derrick L. Turner

Abbott Hall
MSUAA Photo

MSUAA Photo

And thy praises, MSU.

Linton Hall
Tim Potter

Kurt Stepnitz

Harley Seeley

Tim Potter

Engineering Courtyard
Harley Seeley

John A. Hannah Administration Building
Harley Seeley

MSUAA Photo

Hannah

MSUAA Photo

Kresge Art Museum
Tim Potter

Mason/Abbot Hall
Tim Potter

Alumni Memorial Chapel
Tim Potter

Harley Seeley

G.L. Kohuth

When from these scenes we wander ...

Jack Breslin Student Events Center
Harley Seeley

Michigan State University

spring

Tim Potter

G. L. Kohuth

South Campus
G. L. Kohuth

Amanda Ross

G. L. Kohuth

Old Horticulture Hall
Harley Seeley

College of Music
G. L. Kohuth

Tim Potter

Kurt Stepnitz

Tim Potter

And twilight shadows fade, ...

Kurt Stepnitz

Landon Hall
Harley Seeley

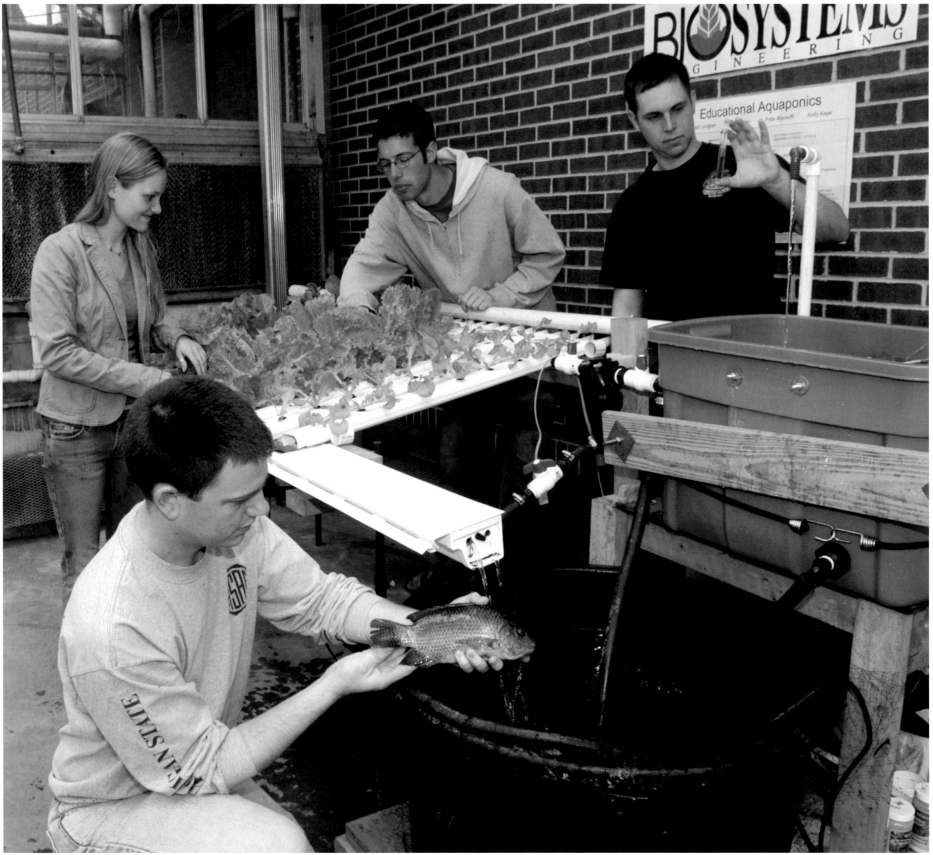

Harley Seeley

G. L. Kohuth

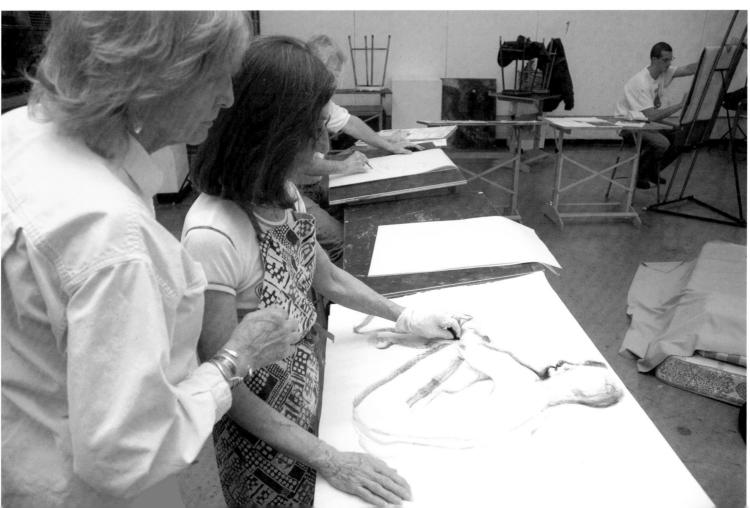

MSUAA Photo

National Ford Safety and Toxicology Center
Erin Doyle Groom

Tim Potter

Linton Hall
Kurt Stepnitz

Harley Seeley

Our mem'ry still will linger ...

Harley Seeley

Harley Seeley

Tim Potter

Biomedical and Physical Sciences Atrium
Kurt Stepnitz

Kurt Stepnitz

Tim Potter

Tim Potter

Where light and shadows played . . .

Horticultural Gardens
Erin Doyle Groom

Student Services and Natural Sciences Building
Kurt Stepnitz

Agriculture Hall
Derrick L. Turner

Tim Potter

Cowles House
Harley Seeley

Engineering Building
Harley Seeley

Landon Hall
Tim Potter

Kurt Stepnitz

Kurt Stepnitz

In the evening oft we'll gather...

G. L. Kohuth

G. L. Kohuth

G. L. Kohuth

Harley Seeley

Forest Akers Golf Course
Harley Seeley

Intramural Outdoor Pool
Harley Seeley

Tim Potter

MICHIGAN STATE UNIVERSITY

summer

MSUAA Photo

Kurt Stepnitz

MSU Library
Brian McNea

Tim Potter

Biomedical Physical Science Building
MSUAA Photo

Michigan 4-H Children's Garden
Erin Doyle Groom

Cammie Cantrell

Magic Bubble Fountains
Erin Doyle Groom

Derrick L. Turner

Southern Astrophysical Research (SOAR) Remote Observing Room
MSUAA Photo

Sing our love for Alma Mater...

MSU Observatory
Harley Seeley

Tim Potter

Tim Potter

Biomedical and Physical Sciences Building
Harley Seeley

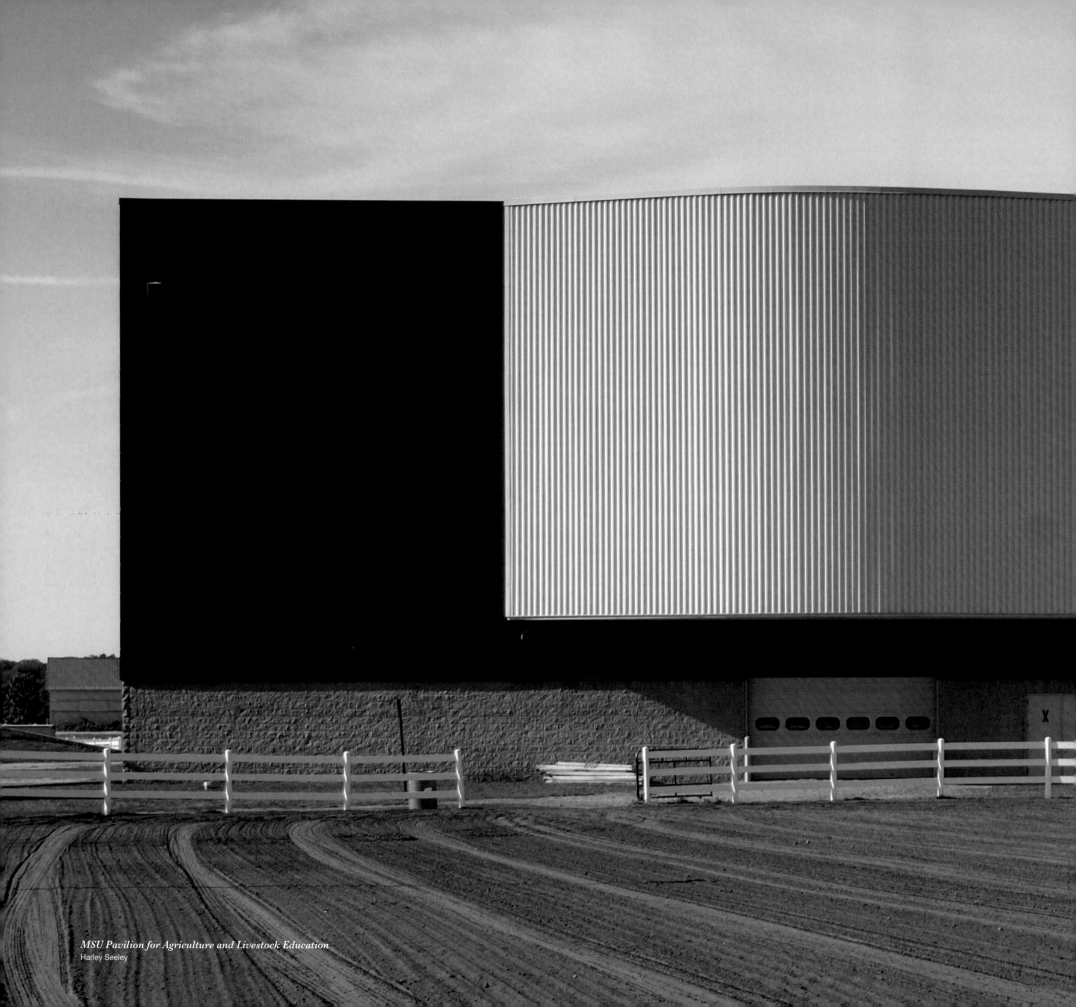

MSU Pavilion for Agriculture and Livestock Education
Harley Seeley

Anthony Hall
Derrick L. Turner

And thy praises, MSU.

MSUAA Photo

Jack Breslin Student Events Center
Erin Doyle Groom

Kurt Stepnitz

Tim Potter

Kurt Stepnitz

G. L. Kohuth

Tim Potter

Radiology Building
Derrick L. Turner

"EVERY TREE SHALL BE MADE TO BEAR
FRUIT AND EVERY PLANT NOURISHMENT."

- THOMAS JEFFERSON

Kurt Stepnitz